McDONNELL DOUGLAS
JETLINERS

McDONNELL DOUGLAS JETLINERS

ROBBIE SHAW

OSPREY
AVIATION

AUTHOR'S NOTE

Since the 1997 takeover of McDonnell Douglas by Boeing, the Seattle manufacturer now refers to aircraft such as the MD-80, DC-10 and MD-11 as Boeing products, even to the extent of labelling them as the Boeing MD-80, etc – indeed, it has already designated the MD-95 the Boeing 717. Boeing has also been quick to claim the plaudits for much of the success of McDonnell Douglas airliners over the years in its press releases! McDonnell Douglas is one of the great names not just in US but world aviation history, and somehow I just cannot bring myself to use the prefix Boeing when discussing such majestic aircraft as the DC-10 and MD-11 – hence all original manufacturer's designations appear in *McDonnell Douglas Jetliners*.

Robbie Shaw
June 1998

EDITOR'S NOTE

To make the Osprey Civil Aircraft series as authoritative as possible, the editor would be interested in hearing from any individual who may have relevant information relating to the aircraft/operators featured in this, or any other, volume published by Osprey Aviation. Similarly, comments on the editorial content of this book would also be most welcome. Please write to Tony Holmes at 10 Prospect Road, Sevenoaks, Kent, TN13 3UA, Great Britain.

FRONT COVER *This immaculate DC-10-30 of AOM French Airlines is seen taxiing for the runway at Gatwick. The airline operates into the London airport thrice weekly on Cubana flights to Havana, its fleet of DC-10s numbering 13 aircraft. Other routes served by AOM's tri-jets include islands in the Caribbean and the Pacific and Indian Oceans*

TITLE PAGE *Formerly known as Northwest Orient Airlines, Northwest Airlines' DC-10 fleet has been expanded in recent years to 38 aircraft, 21 of which are series -40 aircraft*

RIGHT *While most major US carriers have updated their long-haul fleets, Continental Airlines has chosen instead to rely on ageing DC-10s to service its global routes. These veteran tri-jets were photographed at Gatwick being prepared for their return flights to America*

First published in Great Britain in 1998 by Osprey Publishing,
Elms Court, Botley, Oxford, OX2 9LP,

© 1998 Osprey Publishing

ISBN 1 85532 752 X

Edited by Tony Holmes
Page design by Paul Kime

98 99 00 01 02   10 9 8 7 6 5 4 3 2 1

Printed in Hong Kong

CONTENTS

LEFT *Over the years Swissair has been one of
McDonnell Douglas's best customers, having operated
a substantial fleet of its jetliners since the mid-1960s.
This ramp shot, taken in 1993, shows MD-82 HB-INR
being 'cleaned up' prior to taxying out for take-off from
Geneva*

INTRODUCTION

This book features jet airliners bearing the Douglas prefix, ranging from the DC-1 to the MD-11. The name Douglas has been diluted somewhat over the decades, firstly by the 1967 merger with the McDonnell Corporation and, sadly and more recently, the 1997 acquisition of McDonnell-Douglas by Boeing. Already aircraft like the MD-80 series and the MD-11 have been labelled as Boeing products in the Seattle manufacturer's publicity blurbs. The Long Beach plant also faces an uncertain future at the moment following Boeing's decision to phase out production of the MD-80/-90 series twin-jets and the MD-11 following the completion of the few outstanding orders, although production of the MD-95 will proceed, albeit in the guise of the Boeing 717!

THE PISTON ERA

The name Douglas has been synonymous with success in the airliner industry ever since the introduction of the DC-1 in 1933. The 'DC' prefix stands for Douglas Commercial, and it has been used successively on every model from the DC-1 through to the DC-10.

The first – and only – DC-1 was a twin-engined 12-seater monoplane which entered service with Trans World Airlines (TWA), and also served as the unofficial prototype for the successful DC-2 and seemingly ageless DC-3. Slightly larger than its predecessor, the DC-2 seated 14 passengers and entered service in May 1934, again with TWA. In Europe KLM became the DC-2's first overseas customer later that same year, with Swissair following suit in 1935.

The success of the DC-2 was quickly over-shadowed by its replacement, the DC-3, which became unquestionably the most successful airliner ever built. Admittedly, the vast majority of the 10,654 aircraft built were produced initially for wartime service, but many of these machines still soldier on in almost every corner of the world today. The first DC-3 took to the air on 22 December 1935, the aircraft being designed to carry between 24 and 32 passengers, depending on its configuration. Aside from Douglas-built DC-3s, a further 2000+ were produced in the USSR as Lisunov Li-2s and 324 in Japan by Nakajima as the L2D Showa. The DC-3 entered service with American Airlines in June 1936, and it is estimated that there are currently around 1000 still operating on a commercial basis. Some, including a number operated by the South African Air Force, have been given a new lease of life following the fitment of turboprop engines.

Returning to the late 1930s, following the success of the DC-3, a consortium of five major American carriers put together their requirements for a larger longer-range aircraft, the result of which was the DC-4. Douglas produced a pressurised 52 seater which first flew on 21 June 1938, and was dubbed the DC-4E. During the aircraft's flight test programme a number of technical problems became apparent, however, and as these would require additional finance in a climate of global political unrest, the manufacturer elected to produce a simpler variant with an unpressurised fuselage and seating for 42. Thus, the first in a long and successful line of four-engined Douglas airliners was produced.

Even before the first flight of the prototype DC-4A had taken place, both American and United had placed orders for the type. However, these aircraft never reached their intended customers as in the aftermath of the Japanese surprise attack on Pearl Harbor on 7 December 1941, the USAAC lay claim to all aircraft then in production. Designated the C-54 Skymaster in military service, over 1000 examples were produced before war's end, and a great many of these went on to serve with airlines around the world – Douglas went on to produce a further 79 examples specifically for the airline market following VJ-Day. Production of the DC-4 is reported to have totalled 1315 examples, of which only about 40 remain in use – primarily in Central and North America, with a handful in Africa. Of those still flying, a large number have been converted into water bombers by companies in North America.

Canadair also built the DC-4 under licence as the North Star, this variant being powered by Rolls-Royce engines – those used by BOAC were christened Argonauts.

Even before the end of the war, a number of American-based airlines had identified their future requirements in respect to the aircraft type they wished to see built. Foremost on their 'wish lists' was an airliner that could carry more passengers even longer distances – preferably transcontinental. Douglas' answer was a further development of the DC-4, namely the DC-6. This aircraft used the same wing as its predecessor, but with more powerful engines, mated to a lengthened, pressurised, fuselage which initially featured seating for 52 passengers, although ultimately boasted space for a maximum of 102 in the DC-6B variant.

The prototype DC-6 flew in February 1946, and production aircraft began entering service just over a year later (with American and United Airlines). The standard aircraft was followed down the production line by the DC-6A, which featured an extended fuselage, but was primarily used as a freighter. Its airliner equivalent was designated the DC-6B, and this proved to the most popular variant by far, serving with many major airlines around the world. It also had a transatlantic capability, and can be credited with helping to create the demand for mass air travel between North America and Europe. The final variant in the DC-6 family was -6C, which was

United Parcel Service is currently the world's largest DC-8 operator with 49 aircraft in service. All are series -70 jets – a mixture of -71 and -73F(AF) variants. With the recent introduction of the Boeing 767 into UPS service, the DC-8's sojourns abroad have been reduced significantly, although the veteran airliner is still used extensively within the USA, including Alaska and Hawaii. Indeed, DC-8-73F(AF) N836UP was photographed taxying at Honolulu after an early morning arrival

built in combi/quick-change configuration for the transportation of either cargo or passengers, or a combination of both. It could be said that Douglas was ahead of its time in producing this variant, as today most manufacturers offer a combi version of their airliner to customers.

The DC-6 also served in large numbers with the US military as the C-118 Liftmaster (USAF) and R6D (US Navy/Marine Corps). Production ceased in 1958 after 654 examples had been built, and today some 40/50 remain in service. Roughly half of this number can be found in Alaska, 13 being owned by Northern Air Cargo – the world's largest operator of the type.

Further development of the basic DC-4/DC-6 concept by Douglas resulted in an aircraft with more powerful engines and an even greater range due to the fitment of larger fuel tanks. Designated the DC-7, the aircraft could offer prospective operators the ability to schedule non-stop transcontinental services at all times, rather than when tailwinds were favourable as was the case with the DC-6. Seating capacity ranged from 95 to 105 passengers. The maiden flight of the prototype was completed on 18 May

1953, and American Airlines commenced operations with the aircraft just over six months later.

Following on from the basic DC-7 was the DC-7B, which had a greater range due to additional wing tanks. It was this aircraft which, in June 1955, inaugurated the first non-stop New York–London service with Pan-American, although during the winter headwinds often forced the aircraft to divert to places like Gander, in Newfoundland, or Shannon, in Ireland, to pick up fuel. The remedy to this problem was effected by a further increase in fuselage length, as well as wing span, made possible through the employment of to more powerful variant of the Curtiss-Wright radial engine. With more room for fuel, this new variant had a truly intercontinental range, which is undoubtedly why it was officially called the DC-7C Seven Seas by Douglas. Pan American was the first of 13 customers for this variant, and SAS used the aircraft to inaugurate the airline's new services over the North Pole from Europe to the Far East.

Today, only a few DC-7s – probably less than ten – remain in service, and all of these are based in the USA. Although only 338 examples were built (considerably less than the DC-6), the DC-7 can take much of the credit for the birth of intercontinental air travel, and certainly paved the way for the jets which were to follow.

ENTER THE JETS

In the two decades after World War 2 the progress in commercial aviation was quite amazing, particularly in the wake of the introduction of jet airliners. Although its series of piston engined airliners enjoyed commercial success, Douglas, like its major competitors Boeing and Lockheed, realised that jet power was the key to the future. Of the 'big three', Boeing clearly stole a march on its rivals by flying the prototype of what was to become the 707 as early as July 1954. Indeed, it was not until June 1955 that Douglas confirmed that it was to proceed with construction of its four-engined long range jet, the DC-8, with receipt of its first order (from Pan American) following soon after — the prototype first flew on 30 May 1958.

The first commercial services operated with the Douglas jetliner were flown by Delta and United almost a year after the 707 had entered service. This reflected the fact that throughout its development, the DC-8 and Douglas were forever following in the shadow of the 707 which, in terms of the number of aircraft built, was by far the most successful of the two designs. Where Douglas did score, however, was in the number of different variants on offer to its customers. The initial production model was the series -10, which was destined primarily for the US domestic market. This was followed by the series -20 and -30, with the latter boasting transatlantic capability. Then followed the series -40 and -50, the latter being built in greater numbers than any other variant.

All of these aircraft featured the same fuselage dimensions, but in a bid to counter sales of the 707 Douglas introduced three models with significantly increased fuselage length and wing span — these were the series -61, -62 and -63. Many DC-8s are still operational today, including a significant number that have been re-engined with more powerful, but quieter, CFM56-2-C5 turbofan engines that resulted in a change of series number to the -71, -72 and -73 respectively. Of the 556 DC-8s built, around 160 are still in use today (mostly as freighters) predominantly in North and South America.

To complement the DC-8, Douglas developed the DC-9 twin-jet initially as a medium range transport aimed primarily at the American domestic market, although during development a change in strategy resulted in the aircraft being reduced in size to take on the short to medium range market in a head-to-head battle with the British BAC One-Eleven and Boeing 737.

Learning from its experience with the DC-8, Douglas intended from the outset to offer a number of variants to suit the requirements of potential customers, and this decision immediately gave the DC-9 the edge over the One-Eleven in several key markets. Project go-ahead was announced in April 1963, and Delta placed an initial order within weeks. First flight of the series -10 took place on 25 February 1965, with the type entering service with Delta in December of that year. It was followed by the DC-9-30, with an increased length and wing span, and the series -40, which featured a further short stretch of the fuselage.

With the availability of more powerful engines in the early 1970s, Douglas introduced the series -50, which was longer still and boasted yet more room for passengers. The designation DC-9-21 was added retrospectively to a batch of ten aircraft for SAS which featured the fuselage of the -10 but the wings of the -30. To cater for the growing number of customers requiring additional capacity Douglas introduced a further increase in fuselage length and wing

span with the unveiling of the series -55 in 1977. However, prior to its service entry, the new aircraft's designation was changed to the Super 80 series, followed by three variants – the -81, -82 and -83, all with identical dimensions.

Due to Douglas's amalgamation with McDonnell, the designation prefix 'MD' was introduced for its new-build airliners in 1983. Around this time it also became apparent to the manufacturer that there was still a demand for an aircraft with the capacity of the DC-9-30 and -50, both of which were no longer in production. Thus, the MD-87 was announced in January 1985, and production examples commenced fare-paying service at the end of 1987.

Featuring the same external dimensions as the MD-81, -82 and -83, but with a revised cabin interior and improved cockpit instrumentation, the MD-88 was launched in January 1986 with a large order from Delta, with whom it entered service in 1988.

Today, the McDonnell-Douglas twin-jet is still very much in production, but in the guise of the MD-90. With the same fuselage dimensions as the MD-80 family (except the shorter MD-87), the MD-90 is easily identifiable by its large IAE V2500 turbofan engines. This variant was launched in November 1989 with another large order from Delta, with whom it entered service in 1995. The next member of MD-90 family was to have been the MD-95, although following McDonnell-Douglas's acquisition by Boeing in 1997, the aircraft is now due to make its maiden flight (in late 1998) as the Boeing 717!

THE BIG TRI-JETS

The DC-10 tri-jet was born from a 1966 requirement issued by American Airlines for a twin-jet 'mini Jumbo'. Due to the lack of a suitable powerplant at the time, the company's design team came up with the tri-jet configuration in the form of the DC-10, which was also rather larger than American had envisaged. Fortunately the customer concurred with the Douglas decision and placed an order for 25 aircraft in February 1968. The prototype DC-10 first flew from Long Beach on 29 August 1970, being powered by three General Electric CF6 turbofan engines. Passenger capacity of the new tri-jet (DC-10 series -10) ranged from around 270 in a mixed configuration up to 380 in an all-economy fit, with the range to complete US transcontinental services. The aircraft entered service with American on 5 August 1971 on the Chicago-Los Angeles route.

As with the previous jetliners produced by Douglas, a number of additional models of DC-10 (such as the series -15 and -20 – the latter was later redesignated the -40) were soon announced. It was the longer range DC-10-30 which proved to be the most popular, however, being built in greater numbers than any other variant. Still later versions included the DC-10-30CF Combi and -30F pure freighter, which was built for the ever expanding Federal Express fleet. The DC-10 also won a tanker/cargo aircraft competition held by the US Air Force which was searching for a type to complement its already sizeable C-135 fleet.

During the early years of its life the DC-10 fought a constant battle for orders with Lockheed's similarly configured L-1011 TriStar, which had been developed at the same time. However, in the end the Douglas tri-jet was the clear winner, with a production run which lasted six years longer than its competitor, and built 446 aircraft compared with just 250 L-1011s. Today, over 400 DC-10s remain in service.

Building on the success of the DC-10, McDonnell-Douglas announced in December 1986 that its next product would be a new tri-jet named the MD-11. It would basically be an updated DC-10, albeit slightly larger and with an increased, the new tri-jet could carry up to 410 passengers in a one-class configuration. At first glance the MD-11 looks just like at DC-10, and from certain angles it is virtually impossible to tell the two apart. The major external differences are the winglets which, in conjunction with other aerodynamic improvements, have increased the tri-jet's range. The use of composite materials in construction have also significantly reduced the weight of the aircraft, which has further improved the MD-11's performance over its predecessor. Indeed, McDonnell-Douglas salesmen were offering prospective customers a 27 per cent improvement in range and a 31 per cent reduction in seat/mile costs when compared with the DC-10. Finally, the installation of modern cockpit avionics permitted the adoption of a two-man crew, thus allowing the flight engineer's position to be dispensed with.

Operators of the DC-10 were seen as the best hope for orders and, like previous products, the manufacturer offered several variants of the MD-11, including Combi and all-freighter versions. Indeed, it was the latter variant which attracted the first order for the aircraft, with Federal Express acting as the launch customer. The prototype first flew on 10 January 1990 (some six months behind schedule), and orders for the aircraft were initially received at a steady rate, with the first production aircraft being delivered to Finnair in November 1990. Before too long, however, it became apparent that the MD-11 was failing to meet its advertised performance figures in respect to the aircraft's range, and this ultimately led to many order cancellations. The manufacturer managed to rectify most of these problems, but the damage had already been done, and few orders for the passenger variants have been received in recent years.

Although the MD-11 cargo variant achieved a number of new sales in 1996/97, Boeing Commercial Airplane Group (BCAG) announced on 3 June 1998 that it was phasing out production of the aircraft after delivery of the final example in February 2000. Insufficient market demand was cited as the primary reason for shutting down the production line, with BCAG possessing just 22 commitments for future MD-11s as of 30 April 1998 – this number comprised firm orders, options and reserves.

Douglas DC-8

Despite the success of their family of four-engined propliners, it soon became apparent to Douglas that the way forward was through the employment of jet engines. As mentioned in the introduction, the company's great rival Boeing had beaten them into this field with their model 367-80, which swiftly evolved into the highly successful 707. It was not until June 1955 – a full 11 months after the Boeing aircraft had first flown – that Douglas announced it was to proceed with its own jetliner, designated the DC-8. When it finally emerged, the new four-engined aircraft bore a strong resemblance to its rival, with its four JT3C turbojet powerplants similarly underslung in pods beneath swept-back wings – although at 30°, the sweep was less than on the 707.

Pan American was the first to place an order for the new Douglas jet, purchasing 20, although this acquisition was perhaps made as a form of insurance should the 20 707s also then on order from Boeing fail to live up to expectations. Several other major US carriers soon followed suit, as did KLM, SAS and Japan Airlines. The prototype duly completed its maiden flight on 30 May 1958, although commercial services did not commence (with Delta and United) until 18 September 1959 – almost a year behind the 707. The initial batch of aircraft were designated series -10s and produced almost exclusively for the American domestic market.

The second aircraft to fly (on 29 November 1958) had JT4A engines for improved take-off performance and was designated the -20. Two variants were also produced primarily for intercontinental services, these being designated series -30 with JT4As and series -40 with Rolls-Royce Conways – maiden flights for these

ABOVE *Formerly known as Kalitta, but now trading under the name of Kalitta American International Airways, this veteran cargo carrier operates from Detroit-Willow Run airport. In recent years its large DC-8 fleet has been augmented through the introduction of both Boeing 747s and Lockheed L-1011 TriStars (most of the latter having been converted to freighters by Marshall of Cambridge). Kalitta American International Airways still operates some 20 DC-8s, including DC-8-51C N805CK, seen here at Willow Run in May 1991*

ABOVE LEFT *Aeromexico acquired five DC-8-51s and used the type primarily on services to North America. Series -51 jet XA-SIA is seen here at Toronto in 1985 looking resplendent in Aeromexico's now long-since defunct livery*

variants took place on 21 February and 23 July 1959 respectively. Pan American inaugurated transatlantic services with the series -30 in April 1960, while Trans Canada, Canadian Pacific and Alitalia followed suit with the -40 months later.

Douglas, meanwhile, continued to develop the DC-8, and with the availability of the new JT3D turbofan, which offered improvements in both thrust and fuel consumption, it was not long before the standard DC-8 fuselage was married to the new Pratt & Whitney powerplant to produce the series -50. Boasting an increased

MTOW (Maximum Take-Off Weight), series -50 production comprised both new-build aircraft and upgraded series -30s.

In April 1961 Douglas announced the availability of the DC-8 Jet Trader, which was a series -50 Combi variant with a forward freight door and reinforced floor. The first customer for this multi-role version was Trans Canada Airlines (now Air Canada). All variants up to the -50 have the same fuselage dimensions, and in production terms the 'ultimate' early model DC-8 was easily the most popular — just 152

RIGHT *Miami airport is a haven for the many DC-8 freighters which ply their trade between Florida and Central and South American destinations on a near-daily basis. This anonymous looking DC-8-51F carried the Venezuelan registration YV-505C and was operated by Midas Airlines, which ceased operations in 1996*

BELOW RIGHT *Affretair was founded in 1965 to operate cargo services between Africa and Europe, and in recent years the Zimbabwe carrier had operated both series -55F and -73 variants of the DC-8. However, in 1997 the last of these was withdrawn from service and the freight business passed on to other carriers. DC-8-55F Z-WSB was photographed in 1994 during one of its then regular visits to Gatwick*

series -10/-20/-30/-40 were built in total, compared with 141 series -50 aircraft.

Upgrading DC-8s was a major money earner for Douglas in the 1960s, as production figures for the period clearly show. Of the 29 series -10 aircraft built, 21 were later converted into series -20s, 11 of which were further upgraded to -50 standard. Three of the -30s were also converted to -50s, while 54 DC-8-50s were modified into Jet Traders.

Sales of the DC-8 certainly lagged behind those of the 707, and although Douglas offered several variants of the aircraft, there was actually little difference in passenger capacity between them as all could carry a maximum of 189 people. To counter this Douglas launched three new variants in 1965 featuring a significant increase in fuselage length. These were the Super 60 Series (the -61, -62 and -63).

The series -62 was the first to fly on 29

August 1966, this version having received only a small increase in length of 2.03 m (6.8 in), which did not boost capacity but meant additional fuel tanks could be fitted. Allied with an increased wing span and aerodynamic improvements, the series -62 had a noticeably longer range. It entered service in May 1967 with SAS, and all-cargo (AF) and Combi (CF) variants were also subsequently produced.

The series -61/-63, meanwhile, both have the same fuselage dimensions, but with a major increase in length by 11.18 m (36.8 in) to an amazing 57.12 m (187.5 in), enabling up to 259 passengers to be carried. The -63 also has the increased wing span of the -62 (1.82 m (6.0 ft)) to improve the aircraft's range. Like the -62, the -63 is also available in AF and CF variants, while the -61 is purely a freighter.

The first DC-8-61 flew on 14 March 1966 and entered service on 25 February 1967, while the -63 completed its maiden flight on 10 April 1967 and carried its first passengers on 27 July 1967. The last DC-8 built (-63) was delivered to SAS in May 1972. The stretched DC-8 was certainly a success, for some 263 aircraft were built – a total not far short of the overall production figure for all the other DC-8 variants.

That is not the end of the story, however, for in 1979 the manufacturer launched a programme to re-engine the stretched series with more powerful, fuel efficient and much quieter environmentally-friendly CFM56 engines, rated at 22,000 lb apiece. The re-engined aircraft are now known as the series -70 family, with the -61 becoming the -71, etc. The first aircraft was converted at Tulsa in 1981, and United Airlines commenced services in April of the following year. A total of 110 aircraft were converted to series -70 standard, almost all of which are currently flying as freighters.

Indeed, of the 270 DC-8s still in service, the vast majority are configured as freighters, operating in North, Central and South America.

Although its head office is at Crawley (right next to Gatwick Airport), African International Airways bases its three DC-8-54F aircraft at Manzini-Matsapha International Airport in Swaziland. One of these, 3D-AFR, is seen here on the runway at Gatwick, although since this photo was taken African International Airways has shifted its London operation to Stansted Airport

PRODUCTION TOTALS

DC-8-10	29
DC-8-20	34
DC-8-30	57
DC-8-40	32
DC-8-50	141
DC-8-61	88
DC-8-62	68
DC-8-63	107
Total	**556**

ABOVE RIGHT *MK Airlines is another DC-8 freight operator which specialises in services between Africa and Europe, yet has its head office within earshot of Gatwick Airport. The airline's aircraft are Ghanaian registered, with the exception of a recently acquired series -62(AF) which carries an Icelandic registration. Although DC-8-55F 9G-MKA is seen at Gatwick in 1996, MK Airlines has followed African International Airways' lead and shifted its London operation to Stansted*

RIGHT *For a short while MK Airlines operated this DC-8-55F on the Nigerian register as 5N-ATZ, although the aircraft has been disposed of since this photograph was taken*

ABOVE LEFT *A total of 88 'stretched' series -61s were built, with an initial launch order for 30 aircraft being placed by United Airlines. This particular DC-8-61 did not serve with United, however, instead being registered as JA8050 by Japan Airlines (JAL) and seeing many years of service with the national carrier. It was eventually transferred to subsidiary Japan Asia Airways in the early 1980s, this carrier having been formed specially by JAL to operate services to the Taiwanese cities of Taipei and Kaoshiung, thereby avoiding any aggravation with the authorities in Beijing. The aircraft was photographed at Naha, on Okinawa, in October 1986*

ABOVE RIGHT *The DC-8 has virtually disappeared from passenger flying, with only a handful left operating with an equally small number of charter operators. The type has, however, found a new lease of life as a freighter – a role in which the type serves in significant numbers. Freighter conversions can leave the jet configured either entirely for cargo (AF) or capable of passenger carriage in combi (CF) fit. Airborne Express operates some 35 series -61, -62 and -63 (AF) aircraft, including -62(AF) N805AX seen here at the point of rotation from runway 13R at Boeing Field*

BELOW RIGHT *MGM Grand Air was formed in 1987 to operate luxurious charter services with lavishly outfitted 727s, 757s and DC-8s. Part of the 'make-over' for the elderly Douglas jets saw MGM Grand Air convert the interior of the DC-8s to seat just 70 passengers. Illustrated at New York's John F Kennedy International Airport in October 1994 is DC-8-62 N802MG. MGM Grand Air ceased operations in 1995*

ABOVE LEFT *Another US charter airline which has recently ceased operations is Rich International Airways, the company having undertaking both domestic and transatlantic work with its fleet of DC-8s and L-1011 TriStars prior to its demise. DC-8-62 N772CA was photographed on touchdown at Gatwick in July 1995*

BELOW *Air Vias formed in 1993 with a pair of 727s to operate charters from Sao Paulo, the Boeing tri-jets being joined by former United Airlines DC-8-62 N8969U the following year. The aircraft was photographed at Rio de Janeiro's Galeao International Airport shortly before the company ceased operations in November 1995*

LEFT *Cargosur was a subsidiary of Spanish carrier Iberia formed in 1988 to undertake cargo services for its parent company with a small fleet of DC-8s. More recently the company has been absorbed back into Iberia, and its jets repainted accordingly. Photographed on approach to Las Palmas airport in 1994 whilst in Cargosur livery, DC-8-62(AF) regularly stops in the Canary Islands to refuel during long-haul services between Spain and South America*

BELOW LEFT *Utilising a pair of DC-8-62(CF)s, Translux International Airlines operates under the name Cargo Lion. Freight flights are regularly flown by the company on behalf of other carriers, including British Airways – this shot of DC-8-62(CF) LX-TLB at Gatwick was taken whilst the jet was operating for the British carrier as flight BAW3571*

ABOVE *After 25 years' service, Rich International Airways was forced to suspend operations in September 1996. As previously mentioned in this chapter, the airline used DC-8s and L-1011 TriStars for American domestic and transatlantic charter work, as well as on contract flights for the US military. DC-8-63 N4935C wears the airline's patriotic red, white and blue cheatline*

LEFT *Aer Turas has operated ad-hoc freight services since it was founded in 1962, this work presently being undertaken by a pair of DC-8-63(AF)s. This particular jet (EI-CAK), seen at Shannon in 1992, has, however, since been disposed of. Aside from its DC-8s, Aer Turas also flies two L-1011 TriStars on passenger services for other carriers*

BELOW LEFT *This view of Arrow Air's DC-8-63(AF) N345JW about to land at Glasgow amply demon-strates the pencil-shaped elongated fuselage. This photograph was taken early in 1995 whilst the aircraft was operating a weekly freight service from Sweden to the USA on behalf of British Airways*

RIGHT *One of the most colourful schemes to adorn a DC-8 in recent years was that worn by DC-8-73 F-GDRM of Air D'Evasions. This short-lived ad-hoc charter company was formed in 1992 and operated the aircraft in a one-class, 246 passengers, configuration*

BELOW RIGHT *Only a small number of DC-8-62s were converted to series -72 standard, powered by CFM56 engines. One of these was HZ-HM11, which is presently operated by Saudi Arabian Airlines on behalf of the Saudi Royal Family. It is seen here on approach to London Heathrow in 1992 whilst still registered as HZ-MS11*

FAR RIGHT *Emery Worldwide Airlines operates a fleet of almost 40 DC-8 freighters alongside its 727s on freight services throughout the USA. The airline also performs limited services outside North America, flying into a handful of European airports including Brussels, where DC-8-71(AF) N8087U was photographed about to land in August 1996*

ABOVE *Long established freight operator Southern Air Transport has been hauling cargo in American skies since 1947. A large proportion of its flying (particularly by its fleet of Lockheed Hercules) involves work for the US military, although the company also operates DC-8s and 747s on commercial work. Southern Air Transport's DC-8 fleet has recently been reduced to just four aircraft, including DC-8-73(AF) N875SJ*

RIGHT *Air Canada began operating the DC-8 in 1960, at which time it was known as Trans Canada Airlines. With increasing numbers of 747s joining the inventory in the late 1970s and early 1980s, the airline converted a number of now surplus DC-8-63s to -73(AF) series configuration to operate its Air Canada Cargo Express service. C-FTIQ was one such aircraft, and it is seen here in July 1987*

ABOVE United Parcel Service (UPS) is presently the world's largest DC-8 operator with a fleet of 49 series -71 and -73(AF) aircraft – almost half the total number in use worldwide. These are operated predominately on US services, with the recently delivered Boeing 767s taking over most of UPS's international routes. Photographed climbing into the crisp Alaskan skies over Anchorage is DC-8-73(AF) N894UP

Douglas DC-9

Following on from the DC-8, Douglas developed the twin-jet DC-9 initially for the medium range market, but then changed its strategy with the early variants in order to concentrate on the shorter range sectors. The design chosen was similar in appearance to the BAC One-Eleven, featuring a low swept wing with rear-mounted engines and a 'T-tail'. Project go-ahead was announced in April 1963 with the DC-9 series -10. This aircraft was really quite small, and when compared with the MD-80s of the late 1970s, its diminutive size becomes readily apparent – indeed, it is affectionately known as the 'pocket rocket' by its pilots.

Powered by a pair of Pratt & Whitney JT8D-5 engines rated at 12,000 lb thrust apiece, this variant could seat around 75 passengers in mixed configuration or 90 in all-economy fit. The prototype completed its maiden flight from Long Beach on 25 February 1965 and entered service with launch customer Delta Airlines in December of that same year.

The DC-9-10 was produced in six different sub-variants, namely the series -11, -12, -14, -15, -15MC and -15RC. Each subsequent model offered an increased MTOW thanks to more powerful JT8D-1 or -7 engines, whilst the -15 also boasted greater fuel capacity. The -15MC was a combi variant, with the suffix denoting Multiple Change, while the -15RC Rapid Change utilised seats affixed to pallets. Both variants had strengthened floors and an upward swinging cargo door in the forward port fuselage.

Initially, sales of the British One-Eleven in the USA were very good, and certainly better than those of the Douglas jet, although from the outset the American manufacturer had planned a family of aircraft with different capacities, and this proved to be a winning formula as, ultimately, the DC-9 dominated the market. A total of 137 series -10 aircraft were built, although that figure would certainly have been much higher were it not for the introduction of the series -30 in early 1965 as a rival for the 737.

This variant was initially designated the -20, with a planned fuselage increase of 2.9 m, but this was later increased to 4.6 m and its

designation changed to the -30. The wing span was increased by 1.22 m and leading edge slats installed to improve take-off performance. Passenger capacity rose to 115 and, like the earlier variant, the -30 was produced in a number of sub-variants – no less than nine models were offered to customers, which was undoubtedly the reason for its success, with 662 aircraft built.

The basic model was the -31, which was first ordered by Eastern Airlines and duly flown on 1 August 1966. The versatile series -32 was offered for sale with a choice of four powerplants, including the 15,500 lb JT8D-15. Two of the -32 variants came equipped with a forward cargo door, namely the -32CF Convertible Freighter and -32F Freighter, with Alitalia becoming the first customer for the latter. The series -33 was also offered in these guises, boasting an increased MTOW, as was a -33RC Rapid Change version.

The DC-9 soon proved popular in Europe, with both KLM and SAS being amongst the first customers for the above mentioned models. The introduction of the DC-9-34 saw yet a further increase in MTOW, while additional fuel tanks in the belly increased the type's range – the -34 was also produced in CF configuration to meet the demand of Spanish carrier Aviaco. The freight door version of the series -32 found favour with the US military as the air force ordered the C-9A Nightingale aeromedical evacuation aircraft and the navy/marine corps acquired the C-9B Skytrain II logistic transport. The USAF, Italian and Kuwaiti air forces also acquired VIP variants.

BELOW *Unlike its larger stablemate the DC-8, only a small number of DC-9s have been converted into freighter configuration. The largest operator of the aircraft in this role is Airborne Express with almost 70 examples in use, most of which are series -30 and -40 aircraft. The company does, however, own a pair of series -15 aircraft, one of which – N925AX – was photographed at Hamilton, Ontario, in May 1995*

Next off the Long Beach production line was the series -41, which was produced specifically at the request of SAS. First flown on 28 November 1967, this was a higher-capacity/shorter-range version of the -30 with its fuselage stretched by 1.88 m to accommodate up to 125 passengers. Although the Scandinavian airline acquired 49 series -41s, the only other customer for this variant was Toa Domestic Airways of Japan (since renamed Japan Air System). Another version built specially for SAS was to follow, the new aircraft being retrospectively allocated the unused -21 designation. First flown on 18 September 1968, the hybrid DC-9 married the fuselage of the series -10 with the wings of the -30, which boasted leading edge slats and double slotted flaps. The combination produced a jetliner with excellent short field performance, thus allowing SAS to operate into small airfields which at the time were served by elderly piston-engined Convair 440s. Only ten series -21s were built, and the first entered service in December 1968.

With to the availability of the 16,000-lb JT8D-17 engine, Douglas took the opportunity to introduce the series -50 with its increased MTOW, range and capacity (up to 139 passengers could be carried). This required a further fuselage 'stretch'

RIGHT *British Midland (BM) acquired its first DC-9 in the latter half of 1976, and ultimately operated a fleet of 14 aircraft. These comprised a mixture of series -14, -15 and -32 jets, all of which have now been disposed of in favour of additional 737s, Fokker 70s and 100s and Airbus A321s. The DC-9s served British Midland well over the years, both domestically and on their ever expanding European network. Christened the* Eugenie Diamond *(all BM DC-9s were named after famous diamonds, and the airline's business class service is known as 'Diamond Class'), DC-9-15 G-BMAC is seen here on final approach to London Heathrow's runway 27L*

to 40.71 m (133 ft 7 in). Launched in July 1973, the first -50 flew on 17 December 1974 and entered service with Swissair in August 1975.

Many industry observers must have wondered just how often Douglas intended to increase the fuselage length of its twin-jet, and it came as no surprise when in October 1977 the DC-9 Super 80 was launched with the fuselage 'stretched' yet again by a further 4.34 m (14 ft 3 in), taking the length to 45.08 m (147 ft 11 in) – almost 50 per cent as long again as the DC-9-10. The Super 80 was offered in three variants, the -81, -82 and -83, and these jets were subsequently re-designated the MD-81, -82 and -83 following the merger with McDonnell, and are described in chapter 3.

PRODUCTION TOTALS	
DC-9-10	137
DC-9-20	10
DC-9-30	662
DC-9-40	71
DC-9-50	96
Total	**976**

LEFT *Formed in 1989, Italy's Fortune Aviation began as an ad-hoc helicopter and business jet charter carrier before moving in to the passenger market in 1991 with the acquisition of a pair of DC-9s, followed by a 737-200 the following year. In January 1994 the company was renamed Noman, although it subsequently ceased operations in February 1997. Adorned in the carrier's distinctive bright red livery is DC-9-15F(RC) I-TIAN*

RIGHT *Continental Airlines became a DC-9 operator in March 1966 when it took delivery of the first aircraft in a batch of series -14 and -15RC jets. The fleet was further boosted in size during the 1980s following the acquisition of Texas International and New York Air in 1982 and 1987 respectively. The airline also operates almost 70 MD-80s, a number of which have been acquired second-hand. Some of the DC-9s were operated for a short time by the company's low cost subsidiary Continental Lite, but this operation proved a dismal failure and was soon wound up. Photographed at Continental's Cleveland hub in 'Lite titles is DC-9-32 N541NY, which, as its registration suggests, is a former New York Air machine*

BELOW RIGHT *Sister-ship to I-TIAN (illustrated on the previous page) is DC-9-15F(RC) I-TIAR, which also served with Fortune Aviation and Noman. Both these aircraft were operated by Air One during 1997, but with increasing numbers of 737s joining the fleet, they were used primarily in a supplemental role, and their disposal is believed to be imminent as this volume went to press. I-TIAR is seen at rest at Rome's Fiumicino Airport in September 1997, the outline of its cargo door in the forward port fuselage skinning being just visible*

BELOW LEFT *Only ten DC-9-21s were produced, all of which were custom-built for SAS. This variant features the same fuselage as the series -10, but with the larger and aero-dynamically improved wings of the series -30, thus giving the jetliner excellent performance for operating out of small airfields previously incapable of receiving jets. This aircraft entered service in December 1968, and four remain in the SAS inventory today. Seen taxying past an MD-87 at Stockholm's Arlanda Airport is OY-KIA Guttorm Viking, this particular jet being the first DC-9-21 built – it was originally registered LN-RLL*

OVERLEAF *In recent years all the major US operators have been making record profits with one exception, Trans World Airlines (TWA). The Sword of Damocles seems to have been hanging over the airline for a number of years now, and the financial uncertainties blighting TWA can in part be blamed on the fact that it operates some of the oldest jets still in service with any of the American 'majors'. Early in 1998 the airline finally pensioned off its ageing L-1011 TriStars and 747s, although at the smaller end of its fleet, TWA still flies a large number of main-tenance intensive and fuel thirsty 727s and DC-9s. One such aircraft is DC-9-31 N976Z, this particular aircraft having started its career with Ozark Airlines over 30 years ago*

RIGHT *Air Canada was an early customer for the DC-9, being the first non US airline to take delivery of the Douglas 'twin'. A total of 15 series -14 and -15 jets were received, examples of the latter variant being acquired secondhand from Continental, followed by 45 larger series -32 aircraft. Despite the introduction of Canadair Regional Jets and Airbus A319s and A320s, most of the DC-9s have been retained as the airline has steadily increased its route network and frequencies, particularly on cross-border US flights. DC-9-32 C-FTLR is seen climbing out of Toronto painted in the airline's old livery*

BELOW RIGHT *Dallas-based Express One International currently operates a fleet of some 26 727s, the majority of which are freighters. The airline also flies ad-hoc charters with its passenger equipped aircraft, formerly using a small number of DC-9s and DC-10s in this role. DC-9-32 N946ML is seen taxying to its gate at Toronto in June 1994 having just completed a charter flight*

LEFT *Grand Airways began operations in 1980, but was forced to cease business in January 1996. During its final year of operation the airline employed three leased DC-9-32s to carry passengers to its ever popular Las Vegas base. Photographed clearing the runway at Phoenix Sky Harbor Airport in March 1995 is series -32 jet N5342L*

RIGHT *Aeromexico's busy schedule of flights into Los Angeles is usually carried out by its large fleet of MD-80s, so the sight of one of the carrier's older DC-9-32s (XA-DEJ in this instance) on approach to the Californian airport is rather a rare one. The airline operates four of the five variants of the MD-80 family, with the MD-81 being the odd one out*

BELOW *Belying its 25 years of service, DC-9-32 C-FTMT looks resplendent in Air Canada's current livery in this June 1997 shot*

ABOVE *Like SAS, Alitalia has been a long and valued customer of the Douglas Company, and like its Scandinavian counterpart, has taken delivery of substantial numbers of DC-9s and MD-80s. Alitalia has operated 58 different DC-9s over the years, although the last of these has now been disposed of in favour of far younger MD-82s. For ground handling crews the DC-9 is an easy aircraft to work with, as the baggage holds are accessible from ground level, as demon-strated by this head-on shot of DC-9-32 I-RIFU*

BELOW *Aviaco once exclusively operated within Spain, although the Iberia subsidiary has in recent years began to service a number of international destinations for its parent company as well. Its fleet of DC-9s includes a number of former Iberia aircraft, including series -32 jet EC-BYJ, seen here about to land at Las Palmas. The airline also operates 13 MD-88s, which were the first to appear in Europe. However, due to recent fleet and route rationalisation, Aviaco may soon loose its identity and become completely absorbed by its parent company*

LEFT *Produced at the request of SAS, the series -41 variant of the DC-9 was a higher capacity, but shorter range, version of the popular series -30, featuring a small increase in fuselage length. The Scandinavian airline ultimately acquired 49 examples of this model for domestic services, 24 of which are still currently in use – the type is now also used on some international services. This photograph of DC-9-41 SE-DDS Alrik Viking reveals its undercarriage in the final stages of retraction as the jet climbs out of Copenhagen's Kastrup Airport, heading for the Norwegian capital of Oslo*

BELOW LEFT *The large flaps on the moving tailplane of the DC-9 are clearly visible on this SAS series -41 parked on the ramp at Copenhagen*

RIGHT *Nordic East Airlines is a small Swedish charter company which commenced operations from Stockholm in 1991. It acquired both an MD-82 and a DC-9-41 on lease from SAS to fulfil its service, the latter aircraft being OY-KGH, which was re-registered SE-DLC and christened City of Stockholm. These aircraft have now been disposed of in favour of pairs of 737s and L-1011 TriStars, the enlarging of the fleet coinciding with the company subtly changing its name to Nordic European Airlines*

BELOW RIGHT *Hawaiian Air's stunning livery would look good on any aircraft, but it is shown to excellent effect on sleek DC-9-51 N679HA – this former Swissair example was actually the 850th DC-9 built.. Having operated a number of different DC-9 variants over the years, the airline has standardised on the series -51 of late, and now utilises a fleet of 13 such aircraft on its inter-island network. The airline also uses DC-10s leased from American Airlines for its long haul transpacific services*

LEFT *Following in the wake of the name change from Toa Domestic Airlines (TDA) to Japan Air System (JAS) in April 1988, the 'new' company marked its establishment with the introduction of a colourful white, yellow, red and dark blue livery. Since then JAS's DC-9s have been sold to Airborne Express and converted into freighters, with their place being taken by MD-81s and -87s. The airline has also acquired 16 MD-90s, while its large Airbus A300 fleet has been supplemented by two DC-10s and two (from an order for seven) Boeing 777s. The bright sunshine at Nagoya displays the JAS livery to good effect on DC-9-41 JA8440*

OVERLEAF *The only other customer for the DC-9-41 was TDA, which took delivery of the first of 22 aircraft in March 1974. The airline fitted these jets out for 128 seats in a one-class cabin, whereas SAS opted for 105 seats in a mixed business/economy config-uration. Seen in TDA livery on the taxyway at Naha, Okinawa, in September 1986 is DC-9-41 JA8449*

RIGHT *Gone but not forgotten. Republic Airlines was once one of the biggest carriers in the USA, and, during the early 1980s, the largest DC-9 operator in the world. Formed as a result of a July 1979 merger between North Central and Southern Airways, Republic's fleet and network expanded further still with the acquisition in 1980 of Hughes Airwest. Following yet another merger, this time with Northwest Airlines, in 1986, Republic's identity dis-appeared and its fleet of Douglas twin-jets were repainted in the famous red and grey livery of its new owners. Photographed at Toronto only a matter of months prior to the merger is DC-9-51 N787NC*

LEFT *Repainted in North-west Airline's distinctive scheme, DC-9-51 N775NC was one of the Douglas 'twins' acquired by the company following the 1986 merger. This aircraft had originally commenced its career with North Central Airlines, and is presently just one of almost 190 DC-9s (of virtually every variant) operated by Northwest. Following the recent acquisition of Avro RJ100s, it is likely that the airlines will dispose of some of its older and smaller DC-9 variants, this fate perhaps also awaiting other DC-9s as more and more A320s join the inventory. Note the thrust reverser 'buckets' deployed on this aircraft, which was photographed soon after landing at Detroit Metropolitan Airport*

RIGHT *Finnair has operated DC-9s since 1971, and currently has 12 series -51s and 25 MD-82s, -83s and -87s on its books. The days of the DC-9 must surely now be numbered, however, as the airline has placed orders with Airbus for examples of all three members of its single-aisle narrow body family, namely the A319, A320 and A321. Returning to the DC-9s, despite their age, Finnair has always kept its fleet of Douglas 'twins' in immaculate condition, as this photograph of series -51 OH-LYZ clearly shows*

RIGHT *Eurofly operates executive and ad-hoc charter services from Turin with a fleet of business jets such as the Lear Jet, assorted Dassault Falcons and a Gulfstream IV. These aircraft are supported by a pair of DC-9-51s and three MD-83s, both of the older Douglas 'twins' being former Inex-Adria machines which were acquired in November 1989. I-FLYZ displayed the airline's simple livery on a visit to Gatwick*

BELOW RIGHT *Formed by the Aga Khan in 1963 to promote tourism to Sardinia, Alisarda began DC-9 operations with a pair of series -14s in 1974, adding a pair of series -32 aircraft at a later date. The company later progressed to the DC-9-51 and MD-82, and in May 1991 changed its name to Meridiana and implemented several international routes. Four BAe 146s are also utilised on services from Florence, with the Douglas 'twins' looking after most of the other routes. Six DC-9-51s are currently in service, including I-SMEI which is seen here on the taxyway at Rome's Fiumicino Airport*

LEFT City of Buffalo R.I.P. The time comes when, apart from the chosen few displayed in museums, all good aircraft must succumb to the breaker's torch. After countless hours and numerous cycles in the air. this ex-Midway Airlines DC-9 has suffered the ultimate humiliation at the hands of the scrap man at Detroit Willow Run Airport

McDonnell Douglas MD-80/-90

BELOW *MD-81, -82 and -83 series jetliners have proven to be extremely popular with US airlines yet, strangely, none operate north of the border in Canada. Alaska Airlines has been flying MD-80s since the mid 1980s, and currently operates some 41 MD-82/-83 aircraft alongside its 737s. The MD-80s are used predominantly on the US west coast from Alaska in the north to San Diego in the south, with Los Angeles and Seattle being the largest hubs. Despite its name, Alaska Airlines is based at Seattle, where MD-82 N956AS is seen with the Olympic Mountains in the background*

Following the merger with McDonnell, the new company decided in 1983 to re-designate the DC-9 Super 80 series (which included the -81, -82 and -83) the MD-81, MD-82 and MD-83. All three variants share the same external dimensions, with seating for up to 172 passengers, and the new series was launched in 1977 with orders from Austrian Airlines and Swissair.

The first to fly was an MD-81 on 18 October 1979, and the type entered service with Swissair on 5 October 1980. Next along the production line was the MD-82, which featured more powerful engines – ideal for hot and high operations – and a small increase in range. The first of these flew on 8 January 1981, and the type entered service with Republic Airlines soon

afterwards. With a strengthened undercarriage and additional fuel tanks, the MD-83 was the long-range variant of the family, and it was launched in January 1983. The prototype took to the skies on 17 December 1984 and entered service with Alaska Airlines just two months later.

In April 1985 McDonnell Douglas signed a significant agreement with the Shanghai Aviation Industrial Corporation (SAIC) which saw the company secure assembly rights for a batch of MD-82s supplied as components and sub-assemblies shipped from the USA and destined for Chinese carriers .

Due to demand from the airlines for a modern 'MD twin-jet' with the capacity of DC-9 series -30 and -50 aircraft, the manufacturer launched the MD-87 in January 1985, which

utilised a fuselage shortened by 5 m (16 ft 5 in) that could accommodate up to 139 passengers – it also has a slightly larger tail fin. The first MD-87 flew on 4 December 1986 and the type entered service with Austrian Airlines just over a year later. Only 75 examples of this variant were built, however, and most of these serve in Europe. Some have also been delivered to corporate customers like the Ford Motor Company in Europe.

Next in the manufacturer's twin-jet portfolio was the MD-88, which was announced in January 1986. This aircraft is basically an updated MD-82, with the manufacturer making more use of composite materials in its construction. Sharing the same dimension as its earlier cousins, the MD-88 has a revised cabin interior with a wider aisle and improved cockpit instrumentation. Although McDonnell Douglas had high hopes for this variant on the back of an order for 80 aircraft from Delta Airlines, only a handful of additional customers have received this variant. The first MD-88 flew on 15 August

1987, and the type entered service with Delta the following January – the first eight examples delivered to the airline were MD-82s suitably modified and fitted with more powerful JT8D-219 engines.

In 1987 McDonnell Douglas began experimental trials of the MD-81UHB, the suffix standing for Ultra-High-Bypass, which denoted the fitment of the General Electric GE36 UHB engine mounted on the port side. This engine was initially configured with two eight bladed fans, but was later changed to a configuration of a ten bladed fan in front and an eight bladed fan at the rear. Tests showed that this engine produced significant fuel savings, and the aircraft visited the SBAC Farnborough show in order to drum up support. However, the production of more fuel efficient turbofan engines eventually killed off the idea.

Next to emerge from the design office at Long Beach was the MD-90, which was launched in November 1989 following receipt of a large order again from Delta. The MD-90 has a

ABOVE *American Airlines has the distinction of owning the world's largest fleet of MD-80 series jetliners, operating an amazing 260 MD-82/-83s. These are without a doubt the workhorse of the airline's domestic route network, and can be seen at most major airports throughout the USA. Seen here with its landing gear retracting, MD-82 N3515 departs Seattle-Tacoma International Airport*

slightly increased fuselage length and further design refinements made to the cabin and flight deck instrumentation. The MD-90 is easily identifiable due to its powerful and large V2500 engines, the prototype, designated the MD-90-30, making its maiden flight on 22 February 1993 and the first production jet commencing service with Delta in April 1995. The aircraft is also to be produced in China by SAIC, and US-built examples have already entered service with China Eastern and China Northern Airlines. Other Asian operators include Eva Air, Great China and Uni-Air, in Taiwan, and Japan Air System. A total of 131 aircraft have been ordered, and the aircraft is also in service with Reno Air and SAS. Plans for an increased range variant known as the MD-90-50 have been dropped, however.

Whilst most manufacturers have been looking at, and building, bigger aircraft, McDonnell Douglas bucked the trend by focusing on the 100-seat market for its next project, designated the MD-95. In simple terms a 'shrunken' version of the MD-90, the MD-95 was originally scheduled to complete its maiden flight in March 1997. Launch (and so far only) customer is AirTran Airlines, which ordered 50, with options on a further 50, while trading as Valujet.

The programme has slipped somewhat, however, not least because of the uncertainty over its future following the acquisition of McDonnell Douglas by Boeing in 1997. The new owner has now committed itself to the aircraft – albeit in its new guise as the 717-200 (announced in January 1998), and the aircraft was rolled out on 10 June 1998. Boeing is also considering offering the BMW/Rolls-Royce BR715-powered 717 in 80- and 130-seat variants as the -100 and -300 respectively.

Another fall-out of the Boeing take-over is that the Seattle based giant has announced that MD-80 and -90 production will cease as soon as the few outstanding orders have been completed. This could be later than originally anticipated, however, thanks to a surprise order for 24 MD-83s placed by TWA in April 1998.

PRODUCTION TOTALS	
MD-81	132
MD-82	562
MD-83	237 (+32)
MD-87	75
MD-88	158
MD-90	70 (+60)
Total	**1234 (+92 on order)**

LEFT *Although USAir operates a large fleet of ageing DC-9s, it also has 31 ex-Pacific Southwest MD-81s and -82s in service. In 1997 the company changed its name to US Airways, although it will be sometime period of time before all the aircraft in the airline's fleet appear with the new titling. MD-82 N815US was photographed at Toronto in 1997 still in USAir colours*

ABOVE RIGHT ALM Antillean Airlines was formed in 1964 as a subsidiary of KLM, commencing operations with DC-9s leased from the parent company. The venerable Douglas 'twins' were eventually replaced by MD-82s, and three of these currently serve alongside four DHC-8s. Based at Curacao, ALM serves several destinations in the Caribbean, as well as New York and Miami. Photo-graphed at the latter destination in 1990 is leased MD-82 N76823, which was then still wearing its Continental cheatline

RIGHT To supplement its DC-9 fleet, Aeromexico has acquired a 30 MD-80 variants – MD-82s, -83s, -87s and -88s. These can be seen operating into and out of a number of airports in the southern United States including Phoenix, Arizona, from where MD-83 N861LF is seen departing

LEFT Despite the large number of DC-9s operating in South America, few airlines in that continent have found the necessary cash to upgrade to MD-80s. One that has, however, is Avianca of Colombia, which operates 11 Irish registered MD-83s on lease from GPA. These aircraft have largely replaced 727s, and supplement the 757s and 767s on services to the USA. Painted up in Avianca's distinctive orange and white colour scheme, MD-83 EI-CEP was photographed on short finals at Miami in January 1997

RIGHT At the airports of popular holiday resorts in the Mediterranean and Canary Islands, German airliners can be seen in abundance. Aero Lloyd is one of the country's most successful charter operators, and its fleet is presently in a state of transition as its MD-83s are being replaced by Airbus A320s and A321s. Taxying for departure at Las Palmas in March 1994 is MD-83 D-ALLN

BELOW RIGHT Due to the drawn out civil war in the former Yugoslavia, Adria Airways has suffered several years of frustration and uncertainty. During this period the airline's operations were severely curtailed, and a DHC-7 and A320 were damaged during an air attack on Brnik airfield on 28 June 1991. In an effort to gain some much needed revenue, the company frequently leased out its aircraft and crews at extremely attractive rates to carriers in western Europe. Photographed on just such a charter in October 1992 is MD-82 SL-ABB – the 'SL' prefix was to be a short lived one, and it may well have been unofficial, as Slovenia's registration prefix is now 'S5'. Adria has since dispensed with its MD-82s, but still operates a pair of DC-9-32s and three A320s

BELOW LEFT *France's Air Liberté began operations in the charter market in 1988, and during the 1990s it went on to establish itself as a domestic and international scheduled carrier. However, due to intense competition in the domestic market, aided by the quite ridiculous amount of state aid granted to Air France, the airline found itself in financial difficulty in 1996. It was duly rescued by British Airways, who acquired a 70 per cent share in the company and amalgamated its operations with that of TAT – the latter airline lost its identity in the merge. Overdue fleet rationalisations will soon see the number of types operated by the airline halved from six to three, with its eight MD-83s (F-GFZB is seen on a scheduled service at Gatwick in March 1995) being likely casualties*

RIGHT A subsidiary of its parent French company, Air Liberté Tunisia was formed in 1990 to capture a slice of the growing tourism market in the North African country. The airline's livery was based on the parent company, but in the Tunisian national colours of red and white. The airline also utilised MD-83s on lease from Air Liberté, including F-GHED. The airline has since changed its name to Nouvelair Tunisia

BELOW With the change of identity came a change in livery to this blue and white scheme, with the clever use of the sun symbol in the O of the titling. Of the four MD-83s currently in use, F-GHEC is leased from Air Liberte, although three Airbus A320s are on order as replacements

LEFT *Until the very recent acquisition of a few 737s, the present fleet of AOM French Airlines had a distinctive McDonnell-Douglas flavour, comprising 11 MD-83s and 13 DC-10s – the latter serve French dependencies in the Caribbean and Pacific, as well as Havana, Los Angeles and Sydney. The MD-83s are used on both charter and domestic services, including the busy Paris-Nice route. Illustrated at the latter destination, with the city of Nice in the background, is MD-83 F-GGME*

RIGHT *The MD-80 has proven popular with Spanish charter operators over the years, although most of these carriers have only enjoyed a short-lived existence. Palma-based Centennial Airlines was a perfect example, the charter company commencing operations in 1992 with a pair of leased MD-83s, which later doubled to four. The airline then switched its Palma-London/Gatwick service from charter to scheduled status, and MD-83 EC-390 is illustrated at the London airport between flights. Centennial ceased operations in October 1996*

BELOW RIGHT *Proving to be the exception to the rule, Spanish charter airline Spanair has survived the trials and tribulations that have stricken so many of its competitors – in June 1998 the company (in which SAS has a 49 per cent share) celebrated its tenth anniversary. In recent years Spanair has increased its fleet size to number 20 MD-80s and a pair of 767-300ER aircraft. The former jets are a familiar sight at many regional airports in the UK, conveying sun starved holidaymakers to the beaches of Majorca and other destinations in Spain. Threatening skies at Glasgow contrast sharply with Spanair's white livery on MD-83 EC-FXA Sunstar – the airline has a fixation with the sun, as all of its MD-80s are named after solar features, examples including Sunbeam, Sungod and Sunflower, while its radio callsign is 'Sunwing'*

ABOVE *The long, thin, pencil-shaped fuselage of the MD-80 series is evident in this elevated view of an Alitalia MD-82 as it taxies to its gate at Heathrow*

RIGHT *Alitalia is the largest MD-80 operator in Europe, operating a fleet of 90 MD-82s. A number of these jets now bear Alitalia TEAM titling, which is a low cost venture set up by the Italian national carrier to compete with cut price airlines flying into Italy. One such aircraft is MD-82 I-DATP, seen climbing out of Gatwick on its return leg to Italy. The airline has steadily expanded its presence at Gatwick over recent years, operating services to Bologna, Pisa, Rome, Turin and Venice from the London airport. Note the 'McDonnell Douglas Super 80' titling on the port engine cowling of this aircraft*

BELOW RIGHT *Austria Airlines' association with the MD-80 began in 1980 when the type supplemented, and eventually replaced, its modest fleet of DC-9s. Although the airline currently flies just 14 MD-80s, it operates four different models – namely the MD-81, -82, -83 and -87. Some of these will be disposed of in the near future as the carrier builds up its fleet of Airbus A320s and 321s. Inbound to London/Heathrow from Vienna as flight OS451 is MD-81 OE-LDR, which is named Wien after the Austrian capital city*

BELOW *McDonnell Douglas has found it very difficult to sell its MD-80 series to British charter airlines, who generally seem to prefer Boeing products like the 737 and 757. Bristol-based Paramount Airways operated four MD-83s from 1987 during its brief two-year existence, whilst in December of the same year British Island Airways acquired the first of four MD-83s to operate alongside its BAC One-Elevens, although this operation founded due to financial difficulties in 1990. Airtours International was formed in 1991 with five leased MD-83s, but this successful carrier has now graduated to A320s, 321s, 757s and 767s. MD-83 G-RJER is seen about to land at Gatwick*

BELOW RIGHT *Swiss airline Crossair currently leases seven of its eleven-strong MD-80 fleet from fellow Swiss company Balair/CTA, including MD-83 HB-INR, seen here leaving Luton Airport on a football charter. Crossair's fleet is expanding fast, and now numbers some 70 aircraft, comprising Saab 340s and 2000s and Avro RJ85s and RJ100s. Many of the airline's flights are now operated on behalf of Swissair*

BELOW FAR RIGHT *Balair is a long-established Swiss charter operator which commenced services in 1953. Merged with fellow Swiss charter operator CTA in the early 1990s, the airline was renamed Balair/CTA in the wake of the union. As detailed in the previous caption, the carrier's fleet of MD-80s now operates on behalf of, and in the colours of, Crossair. MD-82 HB-INW was photographed in 1994 while still wearing Balair/CTA livery and titles*

LEFT *The Swiss seem to have taken the MD-80 to their hearts, as Edelweiss Air is yet another of the country's airlines which operates the type. Three leased MD-83s are flown on both charter and scheduled services, although these are scheduled to be replaced by a similar number of A320s during the first quarter of 1999. Gaily adorned with its eponymous flower, this Edelweiss MD-83 HB-IKM rotates from Luton's runway on a scheduled service to Zurich*

OVERLEAF *Swissair has been one of the best customers for Long Beach products over the years, having taken delivery of its first DC-9 in July 1966. These were replaced by a sizeable fleet of MD-80s, which have only recently been disposed of following the acquisition of all three members of the Airbus single-aisle family – A319, A320 and A321. This photograph of MD-82 HB-INR, taken at Geneva in 1993, is interesting because it shows the aircraft painted in the long discarded livery of the 1970s and 80s – compare it with the new livery worn by the Fokker 100 parked in the background. The reason why this particular MD-82 was so marked is that it was actually on lease from Balair, whose livery at the time was virtually identical to the old Swissair scheme*

RIGHT *The first MD-80 delivered to a Chinese customer was MD-82 B-2101, which was accepted by CAAC on 12 December 1983. The first of five such aircraft delivered directly from McDonnell Douglas, all subsequent MD-80s taken on charge have been assembled in China by SAIC. China Northern and China Eastern Airlines operate all the MD-82s currently flying in-country, the latter boasts a fleet of 13 such aircraft, including B-2101, which is seen here taxying at Beijing's Capital Airport*

LEFT *China Northern Airlines' MD-82 fleet has now increased in number to 26 aircraft, these being a mixture of US-built and Chinese-assembled machines. The airline is now in the process of taking delivery of MD-90s, with China Eastern following suit. MD-82 B-2146 is seen just seconds away from touchdown on runway 13 at Hong Kong's late lamented Kai Tak Airport*

Norway Airlines began charter operations from Oslo in 1987 with a single 737-300 leased from Air Europe. The latter airline's parent company, Inter-national Leisure Group (ILG), then took over the carrier and renamed it Air Europe Scandinavia, although the new operator was to enjoy the briefest of lives as ILG ceased trading in 1991 due to financial problems. Norway Airlines re-emerged from the liquidators using a fleet of two leased Air Columbus 737-300s, and scheduled services were introduced. The fleet was further expanded through the introduction of MD-83s and -87s leased from Transwede, but in 1992 the airline once again succumbed to financial pressures and ceased operations for good. The airline's attractive livery is shown to good effect here on MD-83 SE-DHB

BELOW RIGHT *Although associated with inter-national carrier China Airlines, Far Eastern Air Transport only operates domestic services. For many years the carrier's workhorse was the 737, but these have now all but been replaced by 12 MD-80s and three 757s, with more of the latter on order. This is a sizeable fleet indeed when one considers the small size of the Taiwan – the longest sector length by jet is just 40 minutes in duration. However, due to the country's hilly terrain and slow ground transportation, a high percentage of the population travel by air – there are almost 100 flights a day between the major cities of Taipei and Kaoshiung! Framed by the remnants of a rainbow, MD-82 B-28021 taxies for departure from Taipei's Sungshan domestic airport*

LEFT *Born twice and died twice. That is the less than successful record enjoyed by Australia's Compass Airlines. The carrier commenced domestic operations in December 1990 with a pair of leased A300s and fares considerably lower than its competitors — not difficult to achieve in a land where the word 'deregulation' did not exist at the time. The fledgling carrier soon had several run-ins with its long-established rivals (Qantas, in particular), and after only a year's flying Compass ceased operations. It re-emerged for a second attempt several years, this time operating leased MD-80s, but once again financial pressures exerted by its much larger rivals quickly led to the demise of Compass once and for all. MD-82 VH-LNJ is seen climbing out of Sydney's Kingsford-Smith Airport into typically clear blue Australian skies*

BELOW LEFT *MD-81 UHB demonstrator N980DC is seen on the runway at Farnborough in September 1988 during its attendance of that year's show. The letters 'UHB' stand for Ultra-High-Bypass, and denote the fitting of a GE36 UHB engine on the port stub pylon. Although the test programme results showed that significant fuel saving could be made with the UHB powerplant, the idea was eventually dropped by McDonnell Douglas*

LEFT *Only 75 MD-87s have been built, with Austrian Airlines serving as the launch customer for the variant. Strangely enough, this model has sold in meagre numbers to the US carriers, but has proven popular in Scandinavia. The crystal clear skies and snow capped mountains at Geneva provide a perfect backdrop for pristine Finnair jet OH-LMB, which is one of three MD-87s operated by the Nordic carrier*

BELOW FAR LEFT *A close-up of the GE36 UHB engine, which proved to be significantly quieter than the JT8D engines fitted as standard to the MD-80 family – reason enough I would have thought for offering UHB-equipped aircraft to potential customers*

BELOW LEFT *As previously mentioned in this chapter, Norway Airlines briefly operated MD-87 SE-DHG alongside two MD-83s – all of which were leased from Transwede. The aircraft was caught on film at Gatwick in July 1987 whilst taxying for departure on a scheduled service to Oslo/Fornebu Airport*

ABOVE RIGHT *Founded initially as a charter operator in 1985, Transwede soon built up its fleet and commenced scheduled services to London/Gatwick from Stockholm in 1991. The airline's MD-82, -83 and -87 aircraft soon became regular sights at the London airport as the airline built up its scheduled service to three flights a day. Fokker 100s were also added to the inventory and utilised on some of the Gatwick schedules – on Sunday mornings as many as five Transwede 100s could be seen sitting side-by-side on the Gatwick ramp, having brought Scandinavian shoppers to England for a weekend break. With thrust reversers deployed MD-87 SE-DHI decelerates after landing on runway 26L at Gatwick*

RIGHT *Following the onset of financial problems in 1996, Transwede underwent major structural changes which brought an alliance with Finnair. The new union also resulted in the latter carrier taking over the Stockholm-Gatwick service. Another change brought on by the merger was the disposal of Transwede's MD-80 fleet and the re-allocation of the Fokker 100s to domestic services. Early in 1998 Braathens provided further financial assistance to Transwede, resulting in it now being a subsidiary of the Norwegian carrier, having been renamed Braathens Swe-den. This particular MD-87 (SE-DHI) was acquired by Spanair in November 1996*

LEFT *SAS Scandinavian Airlines is the largest operator of the MD-87, with some 18 of the type currently appearing on its inventory — the first of these was delivered in September 1988. Bearing the name Margret Viking, SE-DIP taxies to the domestic terminal at Copenhagen's Kastrup Airport*

OVERLEAF *To supplement its growing MD-82/-83 fleet, Spanair now has two former Transwede MD-87s in use on international charter services, primarily to British regional airports. The short fuselage of this model is evident in this photograph of EC-GKF Sundream*

RIGHT *Aerolineas Argentinas operates six MD-88s on regional South American routes such as Buenos Aires-Rio de Janeiro. Photographed at Rio is LV-VBZ, which was delivered to the airline in December 1992*

LEFT *The MD-88 is something of a rarity in Europe, although Aviaco does have a fleet of 13 such aircraft which it acquired between August 1991 and October 1992 to supplement its ageing DC-9s. These aircraft are used predominantly on domestic services, although they have recently started to appear at London/Heathrow operating on behalf of Iberia. Photographed on pushback from the domestic terminal at Madrid/Barajas Airport is MD-88 EC-FPJ, named Ria de Vigo*

RIGHT *Latest MD-88 operator is Turkish charter airline Onur Air, which took delivery of five examples in time for the 1997 summer season. These aircraft are flown in a high-density 172-seat tourist configuration, and supplement the airline's fleet of Airbus types – the A320, A321 and A300. Christened Ece, MD-88 TC-ONN rotates from Gatwick's runway bound for Dalaman, a favourite holiday resort on the Turkish south coast*

BELOW RIGHT *Reno Air operates an all McDonnell Douglas twin-jet fleet, the latest examples of which are five MD-90-30s configured for 148 passengers in mixed class seating. The aircraft illustrated – N902RA – is dedicated to serving southern Californian airports, hence its nickname, the Orange County Flyer*

BELOW FAR RIGHT
Currently in production at Long Beach is the MD-95-30, 131 of which have been ordered to date (20 of these are MD-95-30T Trunkliners for assembly in China). As with the MD-88, Delta is presently the largest operator of the type, with 16 out of an order for 31 delivered to date. The best location in the USA for spotting the MD-90 is Orange County/John Wayne Airport in southern California, the jet's quiet noise signature making it well suited for both Delta and Reno Air operations into the airport – N909DA of the former airline is illustrated

RIGHT At first glance the MD-90 looks just like almost any other member of the MD-80 family, but a quick glance aft reveals its distinctive large-diameter IAE V2500 turbofan engines – easily the quickest way to differentiate it from other Long Beach products. JA004D features a wave type rainbow on a brilliant white fuselage. Elsewhere in Asia the MD-90 is in use with both China Eastern and China Northern Airlines, whilst on Taiwan Eva Air, Great China Airlines and Uni Air all operate the jet

ABOVE FAR RIGHT The prominent V2500 engine which power the MD-90 are seen in close-up on this JAS jet

BELOW The MD-90-30 aircraft of Japan Air System are, without a doubt, some of the most colourful McDonnell Douglas jetliners flying anywhere in the world today. These aircraft appear in a number of different schemes featuring rainbows, with JA001D (seen at Osaka's Itami domestic airport) displaying a turquoise and white scheme, bisected by a rainbow. JAS received the first of 16 MD-90-30s in June 1995

McDonnell Douglas DC-10

Hawaiian Air uses 10 DC-10-10s on transpacific services to the idyllic islands. These aircraft are all operating on lease from American Airlines and have replaced the L-1011 TriStars previously operated for many years. As this photograph of DC-10-10 N116AA taxying at Los Angeles shows, Hawaiian Air's livery has simply been superimposed over American Airlines' distinctive natural metal fuselage

The Douglas DC-10 and Lockheed L-1011 TriStar were the world's first wide-bodied tri-jets, and they were developed in response to a requirement issued by American Airlines and other major US carriers for a 'mini Jumbo jet' with transcontinental range. Although American's specifications originally called for a twin-jet, it concurred with the design proposal from Douglas and ordered the DC-10 instead. Lockheed, meanwhile, also opted for the tri-jet layout, which had been preferred from the start by potential customers Eastern and TWA, both of whom opted for the L-1011.

The prototype DC-10 completed its maiden flight from Long Beach on 29 August 1970, and the first variant (the series -10) entered service with American on 5 August 1971. The airline's initial order was for 25 aircraft, with options on a further 25, while United went 10 better by acquiring 30 aircraft and holding options for the same amount again. Powered by General Electric CF6 engines, a total of 131 -10s were built mostly for US customers.

The next variant was the DC-10-20, powered by Pratt & Whitney JT9D engines in response to a request from Northwest Orient Airlines for a longer range version. The first of these flew on 28 February 1972. This variant had a slightly longer fuselage at 55.5 m (182 ft 1 in), while the wing span was increased by 3 m to 50.4 m (165 ft 4 in). More significantly fuel capacity was increased by almost two-thirds and, to cope with the

additional weight, a third main undercarriage bogie was installed in the fuselage belly. Northwest was the only customer for the -20 which, at the airline's insistence, the manufacturer later redesignated the series -40. A few months later in June 1972, the first series -30 took to the skies, and like the series -20, whose physical dimensions it shared, this was a long-range variant powered by General Electric engines.

This version proved extremely popular with airlines all over the world, and 206 examples were eventually built. Despite their advancing age, good DC-10-30s can still command a very high price indeed in today's second-hand market, thus denoting it as being a truly exceptional aircraft. Even British Airways (a Boeing customer through and through) still operates the eight DC-10s it inherited from the take-over of British Caledonian. There is also an extended range (ER) variant of the series -30, which offers an increase in range of some 40 per

cent when compared to the original series -10.

Not to be confused with the Northwest aircraft later so redesignated, the first proper series -40 flew on 25 July 1975 fitted with more powerful Pratt & Whitney JT9D-59A engines – Japan Air Lines proved ultimately to be the only customer for this variant.

Despite the limited success of the -40, the model which actually produced the fewest orders was the series –15, for only seven were built. This version was constructed specially for Aeromexico and Mexicana to operate from the high altitude of Mexico City. It had the same physical dimensions as the DC-10-10, but with the more powerful engines used on the -30. The series -10 and -15 jets are the only DC-10s not to have the third main undercarriage bogie.

Cargo hauling DC-10 variants include the CF Combi and the -30F pure freighter, nine of the latter being built for Federal Express, who took delivery of the first such example on 24 January 1986. FedEx will soon be the world's largest

Like American Airlines, United is slowly disposing of its older DC-10-10s, most of which are going to FedEx where they will ultimately be converted to 'MD-10' specification. United still operates eight DC-10-30s, five of which have recently been converted into pure freighters. Taxiing clear of the runway at Seattle-Tacoma in the airline's old colours is DC-10-10 N1811U – this aircraft has recently been placed in storage

BELOW *While most major US carriers update their long haul fleets, Continental Airlines has relied on ageing DC-10s to service its routes. In fact, the airline seems to be actively acquiring secondhand DC-10-30s from across the globe, virtually doubling its fleet of series -30 aircraft to 31 in the past two years. Its six-strong fleet of series -10 aircraft operated by Continental Micronesia is being reduced in numbers, however. Former Condor -30 N59083 was acquired on lease in May 1997 and is seen departing Gatwick, bound for Newark*

operator of the DC-10 as it adds significant numbers of ex-American and United Airlines aircraft to its inventory. The company plans to upgrade many of these aircraft to two-crew configuration by fitting modern avionics like those used in the MD-11 – this modification will result in the aircraft being redesignated 'MD-10s'.

The DC-10 also won a significant order for 60 tanker/cargo aircraft from the US Air Force, the announcement that the McDonnell Douglas product had been selected in preference to the 747 coming on 19 December 1977. Known as the KC-10A Extender in military service, this aircraft is based on the DC-10-30F, with its forward fuselage cargo door. For air-to-air

refuelling the aircraft is fitted with a 'flying boom' similar to that used by the older KC-135, as well as a hose-drum-unit (HDU) which trails a drogue to refuel US Navy and NATO aircraft equipped with probes. The KC-10A also has a refuelling receptacle above the cockpit to facilitate its refuelling in-flight also.

PRODUCTION TOTALS	
DC-10-10	131
DC-10-15	7
DC-10-30	206
DC-10-40	42
KC-10A	60
Total	**446**

LEFT *The return of DC-10s in Laker markings in 1995 was a poignant moment for many industry observers. Unlike his previous low-cost Skytrain operation, this time the entrepreneurial Sir Freddie Laker went up market, offering a business and economy class product on scheduled services from Gatwick, Manchester and Prestwick to Fort Lauderdale and Miami. In a livery modified ever so slightly from its previous incarnation, DC-10-30 N831LA* Columbia *taxies for departure from Gatwick*

OVERLEAF *The name Western Airlines disappeared into the history books following its acquisition by Delta Airlines on 1 April 1987, the company's 727 and DC-10 fleet being amalgamated into Delta ranks. The latter aircraft were soon disposed of, however, as Delta already operated a large fleet of L-1011 TriStars. Photographed about to land at Honolulu in November 1986 is Western Airlines DC-10-10 N914WA*

RIGHT *DC-10-30F(AF) N312FE, seen here departing Anchorage, was amongst the final batch of DC-10s built for Federal Express, now known simply as FedEx. Despite purchasing a large fleet of new-build trijets, the carrier continues to acquire secondhand DC-10s for conversion to 'MD-10s'. The conversion freighter (CF) configuration sees the DC-10's main deck floor strengthened for cargo carriage and the installation of a barrier to protect the crew in case of a load shift in flight. Modernisation of cockpit avionics to replicate those of the MD-11 will reduce the aircrew to two, with the flight engineer becoming redundant*

BELOW LEFT *Sir Freddie Laker's return to the transatlantic market proved to be a troublesome experience for his airline, as it received considerable adverse criticism in the press due to severe delays encountered because of the unreliability of its aircraft. Perhaps he should have done his homework a little better before he acquired his trio of DC-10s on lease, for all three had formerly served with defunct operator Leisure Air, which had been shut down by the FAA for irregular (or non-existent) maintenance on these very aircraft! Although the aircraft had been overhauled prior to seeing service with Laker, years of neglect had taken its toll and several flights were disrupted due to technical malfunctions. These problems were well documented in the tabloid press, and undoubtedly contributed to load factors failing to meet those forecast. Reluctantly, Laker 'pulled the plug' on scheduled services at the end of the 1997 summer season, although he stated at the time that he would restart transatlantic charters come the 1998 summer season. Laker Airways' second DC-10-30, N832LA Endeavour, is seen making a 'greaser' of a landing at Gatwick in December 1996*

RIGHT Like Continental, Northwest Airlines has been scouring the market for additional DC-10s, and in recent years has added eight former Swissair series -30 aircraft to its inventory. It has also just agreed to the purchase of three former Thai International examples, which will take its DC-10 fleet to 41 aircraft, of which 21 are series -40 aircraft delivered new from 1973. Former Swissair DC-10-30 N225NW is seen awaiting departure from Gatwick as flight NW45 to Minneapolis

LEFT *Canadian Pacific commenced DC-10 operations in 1979, by which time it had changed its name to CP Air. Now operating in Canadian Airlines International colours, the DC-10s have been supplemented on long haul services by 747s and 767s. In 1994 the airline switched its London base from Gatwick to Heathrow, where DC-10-30 C-GCPC was photographed on final approach. Like many international carriers, Canadian seems to think that all passengers prefer to fly from Heathrow – but this is most definitely not the case!*

ABOVE *DC-10-30 F-GVPD is adorned in Air Liberté's simple French tri-colour inspired livery, this aircraft being one of three tri-jets operated by the airline. A new livery is expected to be unveiled soon following the company's recent acquisition by British Airways*

RIGHT *DC-10-30 F-GTDH of AOM French airlines is caught at the moment of rotation from Gatwick's runway*

OPPOSITE *The positioning of the centre-bogie is clearly shown in this shot of an AOM DC-10-30*

OPPOSITE *British Airways (BA) inherited its DC-10 fleet following the take-over of popular independent operator British Caledonian in April 1988. Industry sources claim that the airline had intended to dispose of these aircraft, but soon realised what a valuable asset they had acquired, and the eight-strong fleet is still serving a decade later. However, their days are now numbered for the airline recently announced that the tri-jets will be sold in 1999 when replaced by 777s. BA should have no problem finding a buyer for these aircraft, which are commanding high prices in the secondhand market*

ABOVE LEFT *The most appropriately registered DC-10 in existence – G-DCIO* Epping Forest *– is seen 'launching' from its Gatwick base, bound for Atlanta. The aircraft was given this registration while serving with British Caledonian as* Flora McDonald – The Scottish Heroin

LEFT *Monarch Airlines acquired its sole DC-10-30 in March 1996 to supplement its A300 fleet primarily on services to North America from Gatwick, Glasgow and Manchester. Although the sole McDonnell Douglas product in the airline's inventory for two years (Airbus and Boeing types proliferate), the DC-10 was due to be supplemented by an MD-11 leased from World Airways for the 1998 summer season*

RIGHT *A combination of a major co-operation agreement with Swissair and fleet rationalisation finally saw the DC-10 disappear from the Sabena fleet in 1997, the type having served with the Belgian flag carrier since 1973 on its routes to the USA and Africa. This did not signal the end for McDonnell Douglas tri-jets in Sabena colours, however, for a 1998 agreement with fledgling Belgian carrier CityBird has seen the latter acquire a second MD-11 which will operate in Sabena titles on some US services. Photographed at Brussels in its final year of service is DC-10-30 OO-SLG*

BELOW RIGHT *Finnair was the world's first airline to operate the MD-11, the type being selected to replace its DC-10s. Despite the introduction of the new tri-jet, the venerable DC-10s were kept on for a time primarily to service popular charter routes to Palma and the Canary Islands. N345HC, which is seen landing at Las Palmas, was on lease from Express One International at the time this photograph was taken*

LEFT *Swissair's DC-10s were sold off when replaced by their natural successor, the MD-11. The former aircraft had been operating successfully with the airline since December 1972, and eight ex-Swiss jets have since been acquired by Northwest. DC-10-30 HB-IHM is seen at picturesque Geneva in 1991*

ABOVE A Transaero DC-10-30 taxies to the ramp at Hong Kong's Kai Tak Airport as the sun burns off the early morning cloud shrouding Mt Parker, on Hong Kong Island

ABOVE RIGHT Privately owned Russian carrier Transaero Airlines operates three DC-10-30s leased from American Airlines on services to the USA and, more recently, Hong Kong. The airline is proving to be a strong competitor to Aeroflot, and operates other western equipment in the shape of 737s, 757s and 767s. DC-10-30 N140AA is seen on the parallel taxyway at Kai Tak, with Hong Kong Island in the background

LEFT *Since its formation in 1971, Malaysia Airlines has enjoyed phenomenal growth as it has become one of the largest carriers in Asia, operating a fleet of some 120 aircraft – these comprise mainly 737, 747 and 777 aircraft, as well as A330s. The airline also operated DC-10-30s such as 9M-MAT (seen about to land at Kai Tak) for a number of years, although the last of these recently left for pastures new*

One of the newest
members of the DC-10
'club' is DAS Air Cargo who,
after many years of
operating 707s, acquired a
single DC-10-30 airliner in
1995 and had it converted
to freighter configuration in
Italy. A second example has
now joined the fleet, and
they are kept busy
operating alongside the
remaining 707s on routes
between Africa and Europe.
The airline operated into
London/Gatwick for many
years, and both of its
DC-10s are seen during
a late evening turn-round
at the airport

RIGHT With the imposing Lion Rock acting as a dramatic backdrop, Japan Airlines (JAL) DC-10-40 JA8542 turns onto final approach on short finals for runway 13 at Kai Tak. Photographs taken at the now closed Hong Kong airport were some of the most dramatic shot any-where in the world, and it was a location that I visited many times. Sadly, on my last four trips to Kai Tak I did not seen the sun once!

BELOW LEFT Just two airlines – Northwest (Orient) and Japan Airlines – bought the DC-10-40, and this shot shows one of the latter operator's jets (JA8549) about to land at Osaka/Itami Airport. From this angle the ample size of the aircraft's flaps are graphically illustrated. Some of the more observant readers will have no doubt noticed that although this jet is a -40, it does not have a centre-bogie landing gear. This is because a small number of JAL DC-10s are operated on short domestic routes only, and therefore never fly close to their maximum all-up weight, negating the need for the centre-bogie. The latter has been duly removed to save both weight and fuel

BELOW FAR RIGHT Northwest Airlines DC-10 fleet has been expanded to 38 aircraft, 21 of which are series -40s. This variant can be identified by the bulge in the intake of the number two (centre) engine, as seen on N155US on approach to Los Angeles

McDonnell Douglas MD-11

After the success of the DC-10 McDonnell Douglas had high hopes for its immediate successor, the MD-11. This new tri-jet was based on the well proven DC-10 airframe and design, but by using composite materials in its construction, the manufacturer was able to significantly lower the aircraft's weight Aerodynamic improvements and winglets increased the MD-11's range over its predecessor, while the slightly longer fuselage allowed the aircraft to carry between 234 passengers in a three-class cabin and up to a maximum of 410 in a single-class configuration. Finally, the use of modern cockpit avionics made the flight engineer's role redundant.

As expected, the McDonnell Douglas offered the aircraft in several variants, with the pure passenger model being the only one known simply as the MD-11. The other versions on sale all have a cargo capability, and therefore have the

'F' suffix within their designation, followed by a further letter to denote their exact model. For example, the Combi variant is known as the MD-11F(C) and features a 160-in x 102-in cargo door in the port rear fuselage. Capable of carrying up to ten cargo pallets depending on the configuration mix, only five such aircraft have been built to date, and all serve with Alitalia, who also operates three all-passenger aircraft.

The other freighter variants – the MD-11F(AF) pure freighter and MD-11F(CF) convertible all-freighter/all-passenger aircraft – feature a 140-in x 102-in cargo door in the forward port fuselage. The latter aircraft permits operators like Martinair to utilise the tri-jet in a high-density passenger role during the busy summer charter months, while reverting to freighter configuration for the winter. More recently, the manufacturer introduced the ER (extended range) variant, the first of which was delivered to World Airlines in March 1996.

The final version on offer is the MD-11(AH), the suffix standing for Advanced Heavy. Swissair is currently modifying its fleet to this standard (which increases the jet's MTOW to 630,000 lbs) as they rotate through the company's engineering base on heavy maintenance.

The McDonnell Douglas sales teams saw DC-10 operators as the most likely to be interested in the new product, and this was proven to be the case when Federal Express became the launch customer following formal

American Airlines took delivery of the first of 19 MD-11s in February 1991, the type replacing DC-10s on many European routes. However, before too long rumours abounded that the airline was less than happy with the aircraft, which was failing to meet fuel consumption specifications and, consequently, range. Two aircraft were duly leased to newcomer US Africa Airways for a New York-Johannesburg service, although this soon foundered and the aircraft were returned to American. The airline's displeasure with the type seemed to be confirmed when it was announced that over a period of several years the whole fleet would be sold to FedEx and converted into freighters. Although eight have made this transition so far, N1761R (seen here climbing out of Gatwick bound for Dallas/Fort Worth) remains on the transatlantic route

RIGHT *Delta Airlines was slow to take delivery of the 15 MD-11s it had on order, the first two actually being placed in storage at Mojave for a while. Although the premier aircraft was delivered as early as March 1992, it was not until early 1998 that the final MD-11 was accepted by the airline. Delta uses its MD-11s primarily on transpacific services from Portland, Oregon, although examples are also used on thrice daily services to London/Gatwick, where N809DE is seen about to land from Cincinnati – in the background can be seen a sister-ship waiting to depart for Atlanta*

go-ahead being given for the aircraft in December 1986. Other early customers included British Caledonian and Air Europe, although both carriers ceased operations before they could receive their machines – the British Caledonian order for three MD-11s was promptly cancelled by British Airways following its 1988 take-over.

In the wake of the jet's maiden flight from Long Beach on 10 January 1990, the first customer to put the aircraft into service was Finnair, who received its first MD-11 (actually the ninth built) in November 1990. They were quickly followed by Delta and Federal Express.

Within weeks of the prototype completing its first flight, McDonnell Douglas could boast an order book totalling an amazing 340 aircraft, and the future for the MD-11 looked very rosy indeed. However, the storm clouds were gathering already, and it did not take long before rumours of discontent began to emanate from the aircraft's new operators.

It transpired that several carriers – particularly those based in Asia – who had bought the aircraft to operate transpacific routes had found that it was failing to meet McDonnell Douglas's advertised fuel consumption and range figures. This culminated in Korean Air's decision to convert its five aircraft into freighters, followed by mass cancellations from prospective customers.

The manufacturer responded to this criticism by performing modifications (at no cost to the customer) which reduced airframe drag by 3.2 per cent and introducing design improvements to the engine nacelles and intakes. Supplemental fuel tanks were also made available which, when combined with the above mentioned improvements, went some way to stifling the critics, but the damage had already been done, and few new orders have been received for MD-11s in the passenger role.

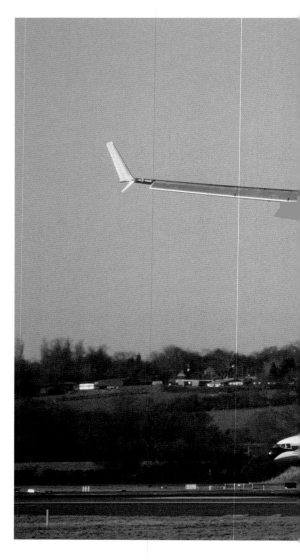

However, the jet has recently found a new lease of life as a freighter, Lufthansa ordering eight.

Following the 1997 take-over by Boeing, the future of the MD-11 was initially assured by the new management, at least in its freighter role, where the aircraft's range and capacity filled a gap in the market for those who do not require, or could afford, the 747F. However, on 3 June 1998 Boeing Commercial Airplane Group President, Ron Woodard, announced that the aircraft was to be phased out of production following delivery of the last example in February 2000. He justified this decision with the following statement, which formed part of a Boeing press release issued on that date;

LEFT *The similarity between the DC-10 and the MD-11 is plainly obvious in this shot of MD-11 N808DE. Even the bulged intake on the centre engine is identical to that fitted to the DC-10-40. Indeed, if the winglets are not visible (as in this view) it can be extremely difficult to tell the difference between the two tri-jets. Note the sticker denoting Delta as 'The Official Airline 1996 Olympic Games'*

'Despite our best marketing efforts, it became clear to us that there simply wasn't enough customer interest in either the passenger or freighter versions of this airplane to justify keeping the production line open. Since our last MD-11 market forecast in November (1997), the demand for the new MD-11 passenger and freighter aircraft has declined.

'We will now turn our attention to completing production of the airplanes on order with the high quality our customers expect, and we will continue to provide world-class support to all MD-11 operators as long as the airplanes are in service. I realise that this is a painful decision for the many employees who have worked long and hard on the MD-11.'

BELOW *German charter airline LTU purchased four MD-11s for services to the USA and the Caribbean, as well as on high-density European charter routes. The airline also operates the 757, 767 and A330, and has decided to standardise its long haul operation with the latter. The MD-11s were therefore offered for sale, and although Gemini Air Cargo thought it had secured them, it was pipped at the last minute by a better offer made by Swissair, who will take delivery of the aircraft at the end of 1998. MD-11 D-AERX is seen sporting LTU's vivid livery on approach to Las Palmas*

PRODUCTION TOTALS	
MD-11	136 (+1)
MD-11F(C)	5
MD-11F(AF/CF)	37 (+13)
Total	**178 (+14 on order)**

LEFT *Brazilian carrier VASP acquired a pair of MD-11s following its awarding of the right to start international services in 1992. It has since increased its fleet to nine jets, with a further example on order, these aircraft being operated in a 325-seat, three-class, configura-tion on services to the USA and Europe. PP-SOW was VASP's first MD-11, and it is seen at Rio de Janeiro/ Galeao International Airport in October 1994*

BELOW *Varig Brazilian Airlines adopted the MD-11 as a replacement for its DC-10s, although fleet rationalisation in an effort to cut costs saw two 747-400s returned to the lessor and the tri-jets retained. Varig increased its MD-11 fleet to nine after acquiring three ex-Garuda machines, including PP-VPP seen here*

BELOW *A member of the Evergreen Group, Eva Air's MD-11 fleet continues to grow. From humble beginnings, the Taiwanese carrier has shown impressive results year after year, the airline deriving a significant percentage of its income from freight, with most of its 747-400s being Combi variants. The Eva Air's MD-11 fleet comprises a mix of airliners and freighters, now numbering three and nine respectively, with a further four freighters on order. In April 1998 Eva Air signed a joint venture with Air Nippon (ANK) on the Taipei-Osaka/Kansai route, which is operated by MD-11 B-16102 in joint venture titles*

LEFT *Like Air France, British Airways and KLM, Swissair has, for political reasons, formed an Asia subsidiary to operate services to Taiwan without incurring the displeasure of Beijing. Two aircraft are marked thus, including HB-IWN seen here in the pleasant surroundings of Geneva*

BELOW LEFT *Swissair has been a long and highly valued customer of Douglas and McDonnell Douglas products, and it therefore came as no great surprise when the airline selected the MD-11 as its replacement for its fleet of DC-10s. It is the largest European operator of the type, with 16 on its inventory and four former LTU examples soon to enter service. However, once the recently ordered A340-600s join the fleet all the MD-11s will be sold off to FedEx for conversion into freighters*

ABOVE FAR LEFT
Shanghai-based China Eastern Airlines operates six MD-11s, one of which is a freighter. They are used on expanding services to the USA, but are also frequently seen at high-density regional destinations including Hong Kong. MD-11 B-2172 was acquired in May 1992 and is operated in a 340-seat business/economy class configuration. The aircraft is seen here ready to depart Beijing/Capital International Airport

ABOVE LEFT Japan Airlines has named its ten-strong fleet of MD-11s after native birds such as the Red Crowned Crane, which is allocated to JA8582

LEFT Like Delta Airlines, the delivery rate of Japan Airlines' MD-11s was rather slow, stretching from November 1993 to May 1997. The first aircraft to enter service was JA8580, featured here against a background dominated by a concrete jungle of tower blocks which can only be Hong Kong. The airline has just introduced the MD-11 on a new Nagoya-London/Heathrow service

The latest MD-11 model to be introduced is the Extended Range (ER) variant, of which only five have been delivered to date – two to World Airways and three to Garuda Indonesia. This shot of Garuda MD-11(ER) PK-GIL on climb out shows off its leading edge slats to good effect

RIGHT *Perhaps the first inkling that some customers were less than happy with the initial performance of the MD-11 came when Korean Air announced that it was to convert all five of its aircraft to freighters not long after they had entered service. Maybe the manufacturer should thank Korean Air for showing the world what an excellent freighter the MD-11 is, as virtually all recent orders for the aircraft have been for the cargo variants. Korean Air's HL7375 is illustrated ready for take-off from runway 13 at Kai Tak while still in use in the passenger role. Note the Garuda DC-10 and Thai MD-11 in the background*

LEFT *Alitalia has been the sole customer to date for the MD-11F(C) Combi variant, five of which are in use alongside three standard passenger aircraft. The airline's Combis are configured to carry 12 first, 24 business and 174 economy class seats, plus freight pallets in the rear cabin. The all-passenger aircraft carry the same number of first and business class seats, but the economy section has space for 215 passengers. Christened Giacomo Puccini, MD-11F(C) I-DUPI is seen flying the spectacular approach to runway 13 at Kai Tak*

*In addition to FeDex, World Airways, Saudia, China Eastern,
Eva Air and Martinair all operate the MD-11F(AF)
all-freighter variant. Martinair's newest MD-11
– PH-MCU – is seen here with additional titles to
commemorate the airline's 40th anniversary.
The Dutch carrier also operates the Convertible (CF)
version within its six-strong MD-11 fleet*